# Moon Poets

## Six Pagan Poets

# Moon Poets

## Six Pagan Poets

## Edited by Trevor Greenfield

MOON
BOOKS

Winchester, UK
Washington, USA

First published by Moon Books, 2014
Moon Books is an imprint of John Hunt Publishing Ltd., Laurel House, Station Approach,
Alresford, Hants, SO24 9JH, UK
office1@jhpbooks.net
www.johnhuntpublishing.com
www.moon-books.net

For distributor details and how to order please visit the 'Ordering' section on our website.

Text copyright: Trevor Greenfield 2013

ISBN: 978 1 78279 617 6

A CIP catalogue record for this book is available from the British Library.

Design: Lee Nash

Printed and bound by CPI Group (UK) Ltd, Croydon, CR0 4YY

We operate a distinctive and ethical publishing philosophy in all
areas of our business, from our global network of authors to
production and worldwide distribution.

# CONTENTS

# Foreword

When I put out a call for poets to contribute to the Moon Books blog back in February 2012, I could hardly have dared to hope for the range and quality of poets that replied. After publishing them regularly month by month, it became increasingly obvious to me that their work should be celebrated in print rather than left to the ephemeral fortune of the Internet, so, here, in this slim volume, are six *Moon Books poets* from the USA and UK. I am immensely proud that Tiffany, Robin, Lorna, Romany, Martin and Beverley have honoured us with their work and allowed us to publish this anthology. If you enjoy their poetry as much as I have enjoyed working with them, then I can promise you pleasure indeed!

*Trevor Greenfield*

# An Introduction to Pagan Poetry

The collection of poets presented here show a diverse array of talents working under the aegis of modern paganism. All of their work has featured regularly on the Moon Books Blog, garnering a positive following amongst readers. The poetry reflects a diverse array of styles, both metred and free verse, and cultural influences. This very diversity raises some interesting questions as to what actually constitutes pagan poetry in the first place.

Amongst the questions we might ask are, is pagan poetry defined by the beliefs of the poet, the subject matter of the poem, or a fusion of both? A poem about an ancient myth could certainly be considered pagan, though if the person writing it is hostile towards pagan spirituality (or utterly bewildered by it) then a great many pagans might be chary of accepting it as suitable for reading at a ritual or other pagan gathering. When Oscar Wilde wrote...

*O goat-foot God of Arcady!*
*This modern world is grey and old,*
*And what remains to us of thee?*

...did he write a pagan poem? Whilst he was an enormous admirer of the Classics, I doubt he would have considered himself pagan and perhaps not have felt overmuch kinship with the people attending an average pub moot.

Equally an ardently pagan poet might write verses about the joys of cheese, which wouldn't necessarily pass muster as a pagan poem. So perhaps we can conclude that a fusion of poet and topic are needed.

Of course the issue of what constitutes a pagan topic is scarcely without controversy, given that five pagans in a room will come up with a dozen different interpretations of what classes as paganism in the first place. Some examples are obvious – such as devotionals to assorted ancient gods and goddesses. Some are maybe more a question of subjective interpretation, such as paeans to nature written from a certain philosophical stance which imbues them with an aura that makes them distinct from nature poetry written by Christians, Rationalists, Jews etc. Others could be story-poems or autobiographical reflections on rituals, personal revelations, folklore etc.

Some of the works included here were written for use in ritual, others to be read simply for pleasure or to stimulate thought and reflection. We hope you enjoy the works included here and are inspired either to read further, or write your own, or better yet, both!

*Robin Herne*

# Tiffany Chaney

Tiffany Chaney is a poet and artist residing in North Carolina, USA. She received a Bachelor of Arts in creative writing from Salem College in 2009. Her works in poetry and fiction have appeared at Moon Books, Ophelia Street, Pedestal Magazine, Virginia Quarterly Review (InstaPoetry) and Thrush Poetry Journal, among others. Her poetry collection Between Blue and Grey won the 2013 Mother Vine Festival Award for Best in Poetry. Discover more about her at tiffanychaney.com.

## When A Christian Kissed A Pagan

Your lips stop signals from satellites
and answer questions I have never raised.
I have found God, again, in the tender
trade, giving, releasing, protective.

I carry your scent on me. So now
you may find me deep in the forest
wet with green decay and longing.
You may have tasted the Goddess in me.

I cannot answer your questions, or dream
even, that you see my perspective on divinity:
Taste passion, pregnant life, heart beating

against you, and my pulse is blessed
with belief as my teeth engrave a more
ancient type of theology on your neck.
The Goddess requires you to remember

a time drumming in your blood, when
both God and Goddess watched us.
Had many names, even when we picked
one patron or matron over the others.

It's what children tend to do when they
want something or get into trouble.
So let us read with our lips as the blind
would, witness the liturgy of the wild wood.

# Circle of the Soul

Wake,
wake the witness,
silent Sulis
of the pond.
Pretend the nameless
are named.
Pretend the formless
are framed.
Wake,
wake the witness.
Wait,
until it is your turn
of the wheel.
Satiate
the self with
the making of souls,
until having played
pretend you can fall
asleep again.
Wake, and witness,
so we may recall.

# My Cailleach

The storm collects a gaggle of old women
knitting nurture for the earth,
to wet the soil for seeds to spread
sprout and flower into small beauties
like the old women before they built
the stepping stones.

The Cailleach is said to be an old hag
that turns to stone on Beltaine,
blooming into a frozen dryad, then
preceding the winter months
when the harvest is reaped,
weathered she is released from stone,
wizened and wild.

She stands on every mountain,
but I think she is the storm
clouds that gather matching
mist to the blue of the rocky
stepping stones, and there
she retraces the steps
of an ancient dance
around the bonfire,
bellowing sheets of ice.

My Cailleach, ancient grandmother,
believes me to be her mountain.
She herds the wild-eyed deer
from field to field, strikes her staff
between my knees so I can't move.
She is gray and bays,
spring windstorms between leaves,
the white wolf calling to the winter moon.
She cries for me.
I never see her face.

## Stitches

When all you have to piece together
your past is a bit of twigs and animal sinew
you become skilled at stitching the wounded.

Perhaps you made the virgin crouch in the bushes
so she's not raped by some misguided snake,
or made her don the animal skins of the slain
to keep at bay the weather and to remember
what it is to hunger for something outside the self.

Perhaps you forgot what it was like
to chase butterflies from bud to bloom,
watch them sleep in their cocoons, but recall
their death three days after the first change.
You danced with the dryads from spring to fall,
and in winter you hardened with the rest.
Your tummy ripening like a plum, the Oak King bearing
spring forward and the butterflies innumerable.

You had to tend to the saplings, let the birds
have their fill of the berries and let the weary
give themselves again to the earth, and how you cried.
How your tears cut rivers into the earth until the land
split first in two, then into pieces. You got your first wrinkles.
The job of a mother never ends...
     Keeping the order where you can.

You learn as you get older how to stitch the pieces,
call back the virgin you may have lost in the woods,
and she'll teach the mother in you to dance again,
while the crone, well, she's just watching you, waiting
to give herself back to the soil. Don't worry.
She will show you how to remove the stitches.

## Assumptions Are Dangerous, Traveler

You petulant prick, preach my sins to save your own skin? I have thighs that crush empires, and you have been lucky to be embraced by them. Be prepared for a sacking because this Goddess-Queen is royally pissed. Your right is to not ravage my heart with your bull shit.

Some swine are not good for the consumption of the soul. Your silence is a petty pretense for your fear. Measure you fear against the shattered crack in the mirror of your visage, the one you smashed because you know it is a lie. Trace the fault lines, those ways of parting and the magma become obsidian, shining black lava cooled. I see the fossils of ashes, in cities and lands burned beneath a touch you were too afraid to give.

Claim not the lands of my heart, which you may not cut nor carve your maps upon. Bear me gifts and speak to me as the Goddess-Queen I am, for I do not reign over any body but my own. Take heed what you think you can do to me. Assumptions are dangerous, traveler.

# Unapologetic

I am unapologetic for
my open heart
my expressive nature.

I am unapologetic.
I gave, I forgave
to surrender,
      to sabotage the self
      to resurrect the self.

Bleeding out flood
heavy the stunned
numb and nameless
need to stay "Safe."

Ma'at
will have none of that.

I am unapologetic for
the uneven scales. No,
I will not polish them.

My heart is the measure
against the feather:
executioner, healer,
lover, teacher, fighter.
Fuck "Safe."

Ma'at, I surrender
this sacred heart
into your capable hands
as you offer me,
again, to myself.

## Harmony for the Flower Fiddler

Flower Fiddler
strikes the path
with her bow,
singeing the way
in the tall grass.
Sensuous beauty
fear not the touch
of the soft soles
of your feet against
brambles and wayward
roots of the tree, play
the breeze through
the leaves and let
the wild strawberries
hidden in the grass
be the balm for bitten
lips. You will kiss again.
You will touch another
hand with your bright way
of being and recognize
the drummer matching
your steady heartbeat.
Beauty hidden among
the brambles and thorns,
play that wild melody.
We hear you. We see you.
You are sacred and silken,
shining as you sip up the sun.

## She Swells With Him

The Goddess green and glowing will soon bloom
full and lit, that moon-milk skin is sage, what they will name sin
pregnant and no father to be found, rumors will surface of
a boy babe nurturing a corn dolly, reminder of his mother's folly,
but for now she swells and wobbles through the lands
tending them until they are brought to harvest like she
wails in response to the wolf's howl and the Cailleach
comes a'callin, builds a fire in a cave and comforts
this sweet child as regains her strength after the birth
the buck all grown hunts for her until soon the seed calls
and the ancient grandmother again teaches her the steps
of a sacred dance, wraps her in the mantle of the long dark night,
and the sweet maiden bends her first sapling into a bow.

# Triptych

## The Maiden and the Moon

When all is dark and the moon plays
hide-and-seek with the land, the maiden
practices seeing with the eyes of a cat
watches the field mice scurry, her lithe
little hands graze the back of a deer
who leads her to the water; where
she sees herself for the first time:
Her eyes are round as an owl's.
The maiden screeches a wild cry
and is rewarded with Owl's answer.

The flowers she wove into a crown
fall into the water and create ripples.
Her hair spirals down her young form.
She notices her hands and feet, good
for climbing trees, dancing, and leaping
with the deer through the woods.
Her stomach digests wild mushrooms
onions, and herbs; it gurgles, she giggles
and pats it like a drum to the beat of heart.

Her arms grow stronger and longer like her legs.
Her hips curve out like flowers she picks.
She makes skirts to match her favorite petals.
The moon brightens with the maiden
and every night they dance until the sapling
she first climbed as a girl teaches her
how to build her first bow and others
besides the moon ask her to dance.

## The Mother and the Moon

A wisp of light curves like bow
in the dark cradle of the moon.
The autumnal geese aim their V
south for the winter, and so
she knocks an arrow in her own
bow which has weathered
many seasons; no longer
a maiden she needs to eat.

Sometimes it is a deer or a boar
which falls beneath her arrow,
as the field mouse is swallowed
by the snake and fills the fox.
As are the cycles of seasons,
so are the cycles of life and death.
The wisp of life curves inside her
growing arms and legs good
for climbing trees and dancing
beneath the waxing moon.

She births the babe as nature
has long birthed the hills, the lakes,
the animals, and set the stars
deep in the cloaked night.
The mother names these stars
between tight breaths until
in the warm cradle of her arms
she holds her first born child.

The mother watches as her babe
waxes like the growing moon.
She teaches her child what
the seasons have taught her,
and when her babe's legs have
grown long enough to outrun hers,
the mother smiles at the full moon:
a loving face to guide her child.

A wisp of light curves like bow
in the dark cradle of the moon.
The autumnal geese aim their V
south for the winter, and so
she braids her silver hair,
shining like moonlight on snow.

## The Crone and the Moon

The waning crescent flickers
behind swaying branches
of a twisted old oak tree.
The crone's knotted fingers
unbend the boughs of silver
loose from her long braid.

She screeches a shrill sound
which echoes into the night.
Owl twists his head around
and answers her, wide eyes
reflecting memories of yore.

The sapling which taught her
how to use her feet for climbing,
how to use her hands to curve
a bow: has taught her the wisdom
of flexibility, of life and of death:
has taught her the wisdom
of being firm, the shaping
of a staff the way old bones
age into sturdier stuff.

She has wrought the paths
in the fields and over the mountains.
She knows the way. The secret:
There is more than one path.
Her ancient body charts
the seasons, the scars, the stars,
each wrinkle a rivulet of mastery.
She adds more every day,
especially when her bawdy
laughter howls with the winds.

When there is only starlight
in the dark sky, the crone
will walk the long walk
striking the land with her staff,
building mountains, steadying
the legs of mothers as they tremble,
making corn dollies for the children.

She is the revered one, all falls
silent beneath her mantle. If,
you should find her crooked finger
pointed beneath your nose, do not
ignore her wisdom or knock-knock
jokes, or you should find yourself
as the start of her newest riddle.
She is a fierce sight to look upon,
but her smile rivals starlight,
brings back the light of the moon.

## The Blanket of Beira and Winter's Tea

The Cailleach keens a crisp howl, sweeping the autumn leaves off the world's porch. She ungreens the bonny hills and cans summer's squash. Tomatoes are tart in the vinegar glass jars frosted with snowflakes. The dawn rises later every day and the lady begins her Winter's walk with her dogs in the last dark of night. She takes the long walk, stretching the blanket of night behind her. Sometimes the dogs give a bitter frosty bite.

Her staff strikes the land and frost feathers striations of snowflake silk. Tree boughs crack like old achy joints. When she passes your home, be sure to have the hearth raving wild warmth. If an old woman blue in the face knocks at your door, offer her Winter's tea. She is Beira, Queen of Heaven, who built the mountains. Let her regale you with tales of her Winter's walks. She may watch the children while you bring in the last of your grain. She will host tea parties and play with the corn dollies with the children, giving each of them names: Holly, Yarrow, and Bramble Berry.

The dogs will yawn and sleep by the fire. When the day brightens on the first of February, she will show you the logs that will burn the longest and brightest. Yes, offer her Winter's tea and she will share the wisdom of her long walks, how she blankets the world with silence for a season. So let us gather around the hearth and await her visit. Boil the water. Stock the shelves. Steep the herbs. Wrap blankets around the weary soul. Sip patiently.

# Robin Herne

Robin Herne is an educator, poet, storyteller, artist, dog-owner and Druid. A regular speaker and performer at pagan events, he has a passion for ancient mythologies – especially Celtic, Greek and Egyptian. He is the author of *Old Gods, New Druids, Bard Song* and *A Dangerous Place* and has contributed towards a variety of Moon Books anthologies including Paganism 101. He is currently working on more pagan fiction, and one day hopes to fulfil his lifelong dream of writing for the Dr Who TV series. He has also written numerous articles for Pagan magazines and has appeared on radio and in television documentaries. He lives in Suffolk, UK. His public blog can be found at roundtheherne. blogspot.co.uk.

## Little Rabbit

Little Rabbit lies bleeding,
His beloved unheeding
Of the scarlet on the tiles.
    Little Rabbit lies weeping,
    His brief memories seeping
    Whilst his harsh assassin smiles.

Little Rabbit loves him still,
This lord who has caused such ill,
Has worshipped him from afar.
    Little Rabbit gazed, yearning,
    Unrequited love burning,
    Leaves its own soul-searing scar.

Little Rabbit kneels spying,
Beneath his lord's veil prying,
Humble soldier needs to know.
    Little Rabbit blind to pride,
    High Lord wanted no man-bride
    Raging, scorning, lays him low.

Little Rabbit eyes dimming,
Faces in the pool brimming,
Distorted souls reflect true.
    Little Rabbit slips the coil
    Leaves behind such fruitless toil
    From bloody bathhouse soul flew.

Little Rabbit sits dreaming
Whilst turns a full moon's gleaming,
Before King Yan's divine throne.
    Little Rabbit heaven sent
    Ensures now no love unspent
    That no man should die unknown.

Little Rabbit, Tu Er Shen,
Grants the love of men to men,
Brother bucks beneath the pelt.
    Little Rabbit made divine
    Fleshed by such love, yours and mine,
    In each caress he is felt.


*This poem is inspired by the Taoist myth told of a young soldier, Hu Tianbao, who fell madly in love with a pompous government official and took to mooning over him. The official did not notice until the unfortunate day when Hu was caught spying on the dignitary whilst he was in the bathhouse. Enraged, the man had Hu beaten to death for daring to intrude upon a social superior. When the unfortunate soldier arrived before King Yan, judge of the dead, it was deemed that he had died for love and therefore did not belong in Hell. Indeed, Yan appealed to the Celestial Gods who made Hu one of their own. Renamed Tu-Er-Shen, the Rabbit God, he became patron of gay lovers. His cult became prominent in his home province of Fu Jian for a while, and whilst it dwindled dramatically under Communism the Rabbit God does have a few shrines outside of China. He is considered by Taoists to be a rather shy deity who is grateful for all offerings and praise.*

# The First People

Wood-born we are; One-eye sees shape,
Shaves timber true, frees Man from trees.
Sea-hauled driftwood wise Honir hewed
Hard-won sense, hence Lodur warmed sap.
> High ash trunk, shaft straight, shakes the sky,
> Skuld's thread new colour bled to life
> Through elm as she forms the bole borne,
> Bark burnished smooth, heartwood resounds.

From the forests we walk so wise,
Wood lore ingrained shrivels, untrained
Gone like leaves in autumn, echoes
Endure, veined patterns in soil sained.
> Roots are soon forgotten, rotting,
> Replaced with cheaper fare, leaves bare
> Brittle branches poor crib for kin,
> Callow limbs, yet sigh the Land's hymns.

*This short poem, in the Norse hrynhenda metre (well, an approximation thereof), is based on the Heathen myth that the first human man and woman were carved from a washed up ash and elm log respectively.*

## Words for Wuldor

Snow falls fast;    Finally we freeze
As light deepens and dies.
Wolf walks abroad,   White yields to Wuldor,
Paths of paw prints.

Ice shrouds the island,  Life insures itself
What seems to sleep sings,
Sweet lyrics echo soft,  Swoop on chill breezes
Whimpers of wolves midst
 woods.

Archer's eyes encompass, Iron will winnows
Weak from the willing
Strengthening stock –  Strong the impulse:
Faced with final fear, fuck!

Hunting and humping,  Heating the Hall
Ydalir warm in winter,
Thick-pelted,    Frith forming
Wolf Lord weaves his wyrd.


*Wuldor is the probable Anglo-Saxon name of the Norse deity Ullr, god of winter who is traditionally seen as accompanied by wolves. The poem is in the ljóðaháttr metre, used as a song metre by Heathen skalds.*

## The Song of Mr Tumnus

A hundred years of winter,
So it felt.
Once limber branches grow numb and splinter,
Life frozen, unchanging;
Jadis, solitary, the table cleaves
Songless woods sepulchral stand,
Leached of hope, fallen with the leaves,
Veined skeletons spiralling into mulch.
All that was once held so dear
Decayed, dissipated.
We few survivors, tired with fear.
Would Aslan's roar echo
Promise throughout the world?
No lion's thunder stirred me;
It was your greeting that unfurled.
Softly spoken,
Shivering up my spine
Dissolving a century of snow,
Letting our songs entwine.
Quiet but richly echoing
In forest vaults strong,
Arterial lust calling me back from death.
Sighing a Syrinx Song
No lion's panting,
But your breath upon my nape
Melted the Gorgon's indifferent gaze,
And granted our escape.
Warmth flowed to your touch, colour blossoming
I took your hand and we danced up the Spring,
Sometimes you leading,
Sometimes I, trampling winter's sting.
The lion-heat of summer

Cannot come till first
Tumnus tumescent
Quenches his forgotten thirst.
Goat-boy you called me,
And so I am.
No Son of Adam I,
But a Child of Pan.
I tell a different story
Neglected by the Spawn of Man.

*Apologies to Mr Lewis for hijacking his characters for ends that would quite possibly have him spinning in his grave! I thought the Sons of Pan deserved a chance to take centre stage.*

## Setka Waits

Setka waits upon the shore,
Ice blue eyes embrace the joyless sea
Whence resounds his lady's roar.
He remembers that dire day:
The coming of the king, father's glee
At daughter's joy at love's play.

Setka casts thought back on waves,
As umiak slid sleekly to groom's isle,
But found no lords, merely knaves.
Stench recalled from muzzle's store,
Foreshadow of unravelling guile.
Maiden's vows revoked sans thaw.

Setka shivers, recalls rage ~
Shrieking birdmen conjuring storm winds
To blow back their queen to cage;
Father, fearful, casts his pearl
To frozen seas, decency rescinds
Last bonds sliced: blood in sea's swirl.

Setka dived to save, but sank
Amidst fingers forming behemoths,
Ocean maid swept him to bank.
Safe on shore, vengeance called pack –
Old man's blood-debt filling the dogs' troughs,
Sea Goddess sated sinks back.

Setka guards the ocean edge
Where the Fingerless Maiden he meets.
Weed-clogged her hair, his pledge
To comb what she cannot reach,
Warming the whale mother, whose cold teats
Suckle seals on arctic beach.

*The poem tells the story of an Inuit sea goddess, known variously as Sedna or Nuliajuk, and her devoted snow dog Setka. In at least one version of the myth she actually married the dog and between them produced the primary races of humans. An umiak, incidentally, is a type of traditional Inuit rowboat. The metrical form is a one-off created for this poem.*

## Sigyn's Burden

Bound in chains,
Deep in Darkness,
The Aesir sigh,
Yet the Grey Clan waits,

Wolf-child and I
Silently dreaming.
They sing of peace
Grim, unquelled.

Poison torments,
By entrails enslaved,
Laying me low,
Eating my will,

Time drips slow.
Such grief enchains,
What loathsome fate!
Each day dwindling.

Once salvation ceases.
Her humble cup,
May Asgard fall,
Down in wolf drool!

When Sigyn empties
Agony heralds doom
Mire Midgard
Despised sons rise.

Flee from our wrath!
A Sword Age, savage!
We shall out-run wildfire!
Breaking all oaths,

A Wolf Age, fierce,
When Van shrivels
Worlds devouring, searing
Outcasting all kith

We will eat the sun,
Reborn anew,
Purged of Loki's like,
Or lotus dream

Let moon and world quake!
A world refined,
Land of frith
Lamed realm for fearful folk.

*In Norse myth Sigyn is the long-suffering wife of Loki. When he is finally captured by the Aesir and chained to a rock with serpent venom dripping upon him, she stands guard with a bowl to catch the poison. In those moments when she goes to empty the bowl, the venom finds its mark and Loki's writhing causes earthquakes. This is written in fornyrthislag metre.*

## Song of the Wolf Clan

Wolf for wolf is yearning, in our veins burning
The unquenchable urge to be free.
Ghosts of the forest, hear us! Brave men fear us,
Unseen beneath the vast canopy.
Bones formed from archer's bow, blood from aril's glow,
Flesh from the spittle of the First Three.

Den-born we, kin of Vindos,
Haunters of the weald;
Wolf-skinned we, kith of Vindos,
Our oath by blood sealed.

Beast in beast is waiting, for hunger sating,
We hunt down and feast upon our foes.
Each tree our brother, each stream from our mother,
Each contour of the Land our Clann knows.
Fierce is our waking, deep is our dream's aching
Yet gladly we share our feast with crows.

Den-born we, kin of Vindos,
Haunters of the weald;
Wolf-skinned we, kith of Vindos,
Our oath by blood sealed.


*This short poem was written as part of a novel intended as a sort of anthem sung by members of an Ancient British tribal nation whose sacred animal was the wolf. I'm still working on what the tune should be! Vindos is the Ancient British name proposed by linguists for the mythical figure known in Wales as Gwynn the King of the Fairies, and as Fionn the leader of the Fianna warriors in Ireland.*

## The Ghillie-Dhu

Pale moon-skinned, hair pendulous,
Still stands the tree-sire, dreaming
Of the wildwood tenebrous
That echoes through the gleaming.

Fierce runs the boy, hell-hounded
Solace sought from grim kinfolk
Future bleak, grief compounded
Gnarled tree faces fears evoke.

To the forest hideaway
He came, a silvered haven,
Thoughts like toys in disarray
Midst the perch of the raven.

Distant bellows terrorised
Setting birds to flight, cawing.
Breeze-stirred branches mesmerised
Till scarce could hear the roaring.

Birch limbs mournful resounded,
"The beast pursues me, Ghillie!"
The boy pleaded, unfounded
Hopes stillborn within Billy.

"I can't go home anymore,"
Whispered the boy, lip bleeding.
Father's rage truth's guarantor,
Tree stirred to the youth's pleading.

Drunken, brutish, thundering,
Dire sire up the trunk scrambles,
Billy's hopes fast sundering.
The tree stands stiffly, ambles.

Stirs the guardian, uprooting,
Wails the father tumbling
Watches son's life rerouting,
The walls of his world crumbling.

Sings the Ghillie melodic
Of the land in the mountains
Where life will be rhapsodic
His passenger soon made hale.

*Written in ae freislighe metre, this short poem tells the tale of a young man's encounter with a ghillie-dhu, an elemental being from Scottish folklore who guards trees and forest. The ghillie is largely indistinguishable from the leshii of Russian mythology and the ent of Anglo-Saxon myth (so vividly embraced by Tolkien). These large forest-dwelling beings are friendly towards lost children, but can be grimmer towards those who violate the woodland ways. In Gaelic the word ghillie can mean either a trusted male servant or a young lad, so for the purposes of this poem a ghillie-dhu may be either the Dark Servant or the Dark Boy.*

# Wepwawet

Awaken in peace
Beloved of the sun
Awaken in peace
Follower of the moon.

Desert wanderer,
Maker of tracks
In the pathless wastes,
Grey light in a red land.

The door is bolted to me,
Confined within my mind,
Opener of the ways,
Unlock what I cannot.

Let me ride besides you
In the barque of Re,
Worlds open before us.
Danger abounds, my soul yearns!

Howling in the darkness,
I shiver to your hot breath.
Let me be open, let me be open
And live, let me not sleep.

*The Egyptian deity Wepwawet is known as the Opener of the Ways, and stands at the head of the sun god's ship unlocking the doors that lead into Dwat, the Underworld, as the sun goes down in the west, and opening the doors back into the lands of the living as the sun rises in the East. Establishing Egyptian metre is difficult due to uncertainty over precisely how words should be pronounced. However, surviving examples of poetry make use of frequently repeated phrases, much like musical refrains.*

## Lamentation

The hearth is smoored, its warmth draws kin,
Smith's forge lures in pawn of vain sire,
His plan flawed as Goibniu speared skin.
Brewer's win casts dam's pride to pyre.

Comes the one veiled, her hair unseen.
Hides the flame's sheen, this not the time.
His life has failed, cut now the skein,
She begins to keen, tears quicklime.

Ruadan's redness spilt, snows shroud drawn
Delays the dawn. Mother's grief
Made hope wilt, all chance of spring scorn
Summer unborn, an unfurled leaf.

The wind laments, ice seals his tomb
Yet light dispels gloom, her heart heals
Memory's price the flowers bloom
Grave gifts, mourner's plume, life unseals.


*Irish lore credits the goddess Brigit with three sons one of whom, Ruadan (pronounced approximately 'roo-awn'), meets a brutal end. Being one-quarter Fomori he is incited by his father to spy upon the divine blacksmith Goibniu on behalf of the malevolent sea giants. Ruadan attacked the smith, but Goibniu deals a mortal blow. As a result his mother begins to keen (from the Irish word caoineadh), the first example of that style of ritual lamentation in Ireland. As well as the mournful chanting, it is traditional for the keening woman to cover her hair. The practice of keening was railed against by the Church with threats of excommunication in 1631, 1748, and 1800. The practice is probably the partial origin of the banshee legends.*

# Driftwood

Sea air heals, fills lungs ozone rich and fresh with hope
So profound it pulls me far from this place in search.
Solace sought on this lonely shore as waves sand stroke
Ancient beats, such symphony as was heard in Greece –
Far Poseidon melodies sang for wading youths.

Brine swirls, soaking calves, ease brought as old bones flex
   strength,
Time once ice-stiff melts away in warm ocean tides
Age-old fears dissipate – reflected, weakened, solved.
Deep dreamtides ebb and flow, sea currents raise lost needs.
He moves, easeful on green-grey rips, swims to surface.

Proteus dries in the breeze, warming on boulders, beached
We eye each other, gaze sidelong as Apollo
Holds two souls in his gold aegis. Chance before me,
Too late I turn, but bare stone shelf is bleak display:
The bold seal herder dives, he is gone, my mistake.

Day slowly drags, sun fades along with my scant hopes.
Heat fails to touch ash future, sadness drowns all gains,
Harpy doubts snatch at joy, fouling this blind man's mind.
Fierce light may not reveal change, yet soft moon love shows,
Saline darkening, seal-hide ripples, water breaks.

Night reigns. Heat stirs his veins to pulse, lids open wide,
He smiles, my lips wet, part, respond with sleeper's hope.
Need grows, tasting of seaside holidays: salt-sweet
Beneath the sun, where seas hide hungers rising at
Moon tide to walk upon beaches where sailors dream.

Vast Poseidon, Nerites soft lips recalls ripe,
So I lay in this name-free lad's embrace, was he
Weed-wrapped sage transformed, made lithe and honeyed skin
    glazed?
Maybe he was that Sea Lord's lover, freed from shell?
Tonight he is here, I wake – an end to dull sleep.

*This poem is written in an Ancient Greek metre, the lesser asclepiad, which was primarily used for erotic and sensuous poetry. Proteus was a sea deity known for frequent shape-shifting, and regarded as having special patronage over seals. In this respect he curiously echoes the selkies of Celtic mythology. Nerites was a lover of Poseidon who, in one version of the story, was transformed into a shellfish (possibly a sea snail) by a jealous rival*

# Lorna Smithers

Lorna Smithers is a poet and Druid based in Lancashire. Her work has been published in *Reach Poetry, The Dawntreader, Heroic Fantasy Quarterly, New Myths, Paganism 101* and local magazines. She is a regular performer at literary events. She also leads walks, gives talks and runs creative writing workshops.

## Proud of Preston

Belisama:
Proud of Preston heed my entry
Hear the call of ancient memories
Hearts purloined by Roman sentries
Like a river shining bright.

Proud of Preston born free traders
Made by commerce and hard labour
Merchants gilded artists favored
Like the Brigantes warred in tribes.

Mechanics shift the scene of battle
Raise the red brick smog industrial
Cording hearts like twisting material
On the wheels of the cotton lords.

Step the Chartists to the engines
Pull the plugs release the tension
The rioters face the sentries
Dye the river dark with blood.

Grey arise the business faceless
Fake fulfillment for the faithless
Mass the market for the tasteless
Selling life for capital.

High in the stone fortress
The sentries hold their rule
Beyond the mall and office
Do you hear a river call?

Proud of Preston I have carved you
In my sweeping spirit formed you
Through your veins floods dazzling water
My Setantii shining bright.

Will you hearken to my entry
Drown false dreams in ancient memories
Will the proud of Preston
Like a shining river rise?

*Winner of the Preston Guild Poetry Competition 2012

## The Bull of Conflict

*I come from battle and conflict*
*With a shield in my hand;*
*Broken is the helmet*
*By the pushing of spears.*
'Poem referring to Gwyddno and Gwyn ap Nudd' – *The Black
    Book of Carmarthen XXXIII*

On an empty day automata drift
Wending suit shapes through the mist.
Touchless I fade like a symbol unhitched.
The spoils of war quake in the museum.
Piercing the grey wearing horns of a bull
A white warrior blackened and bloodied
Disguises his limp in an infinite gloom,
On his spear leans, softly says:
"My comrades are slain and yet I live.
*I come from battle and conflict.*"

His dire avowal brings howling winds
Chill clutch at my shoulders their lament dins
Of hero light fading from mortal skin.
In glass cabinets swords clash savage,
Raging figures thrash on ragged pages
Chanting the desolate past of ravaged war bands.
With war-torn wisdom, sombrely he whispers
 "These gathered memories to you I give
Gone are the days I crossed this land
*With a shield in my hand.*"

His barrage of sadness barks in my mind
Like hapless hounds on a winter's night.
Fierce their madness, dark their plight
For the perishing souls they collect,
The past's great spirit protect.
Like thundering wind obligation overwhelms me.
The blade of futility threatens to unfasten me.
"How do I cherish and defend these memories
When like the kingdoms of Rheged and Elmet
*Broken is the helmet?"*

I ask the Bull of Conflict.
His tears run bright with the passing of time,
Chariots wheeling in multihued light,
Victims reflected in star lit skies.
He says "this shadow land needs enchantment
To banish the blight of despair.
Nurture the memories with magic
And they'll sing a blessed new year.
Do not be pressed into fear
*By the pushing of spears."*

*First published in *Heroic Fantasy Quarterly* (January 2013)

## Sweet Awen

Sweet Awen
sing me a song
of direction
down hills,
over terraces,
past old mills
and factories.

Sing me a song
of poppies and bees
where the bramble
unbridled roams
hedgerows with ease.

Sing me a song
where the first fruits
are born by the light
of a sun who has never
known war.

Sing me a song
where loss no longer
beats like a smith
at her forge
in the summer's heat.

Sing me the years
that I'll never meet.
Sweet Awen
sing to me
my impossibilities.

## Summer Bright

Lady of the summer heat,
Summer Bright, life of this vale,
I walked within your summer dream
when your streams shone bright
from syke to glittering estuary.

I worshipped at your golden streams,
borne like solder from the burning ground.
Amidst the flowers and bumble bees
I downed my honeyed draught
and laughed with the leaping fish.

And the world will never be the same.
They panned for the fish. All the bees
flew away. They fractured
earth's hot core and spilt her ore,
bringing about these dark and final days.

Belisama, Summer Bright
your name shall be invoked again
on a midsummer's night, beside
a golden stream, yet in this life
your dream may not be seen.

## Take Wing My Queen

*We are the bees of the invisible.*
*We wildly collect the honey of the visible,*
*to store in the great golden hive of the invisible.'*
-Rilke


Let us depart my queen,
sisters kiss farewell to the flowers.
Sink your long tongues
into the obituaries of stamens,
one last taste, forsake the namelessness
of this world ruled by drones.

She who builds creatively
finds no nourishment in nectar grown
on the ramparts of technology,
in the cracks of mechanical arms
snatching endlessly
at the noctilucent hive of the unknown.

Hives empty, baskets heavy,
bearing honey on furred bodies
to a sanctuary of wax and comb,
invisible wisdom to hum
until meadow flowers
recall sweet songs again,

take wing my queen, let us be gone.

# Gwyn's Hall

Summer here and winter there
My longest day your darkest night
Hoar frost drapes your haunted fortress
Whilst swallows ride my glowing sunlight.

Summer here and winter there
My brightest day your longest night
Whilst blackbirds sing my endless fanfare
Crazy owl streaks across your vaunted midnight.

Winter there and summer here
And I between them like the song
That lies unsung between the years
Between your hall and my brief home.

# Caer Pedryvan

I am on the way to Caer Pedryvan
Saying farewell to the poppies and bees.
Red admirals have flown down south.
Tortoiseshells have succumbed to sleep.

I am on the way to Caer Pedryvan
As autumn maples shed their leaves
Yellow and gold in the western rain
To the dent of splashing hoof beats.

I am on the way to Caer Pedryvan
Riding down the lonesome beach.
The crew of Prydwen cast their sails.
My wild white horse swims out to sea.

I am on the way to Caer Pedryvan
Where the cauldron of Annwn's chief
Is warmed by the breath of phantom maidens
Whose fateful shapes shift through my dreams.

I am on the way to Caer Pedryvan
Where of warriors brazen seven remain
To stake my wild white heart to Annwn's king,
My boundless trust to his fair domain.

## Glastonbury Tor

To Gwyn:
On star circled Tor you stand lawless vigil.
Tower swallows cloud in your endless waiting.
Years I have run the edges of your world
Yet quietly my destruction you disdain.
Call to the stars shining out the full moon,
One blast of your horn draws my soul back home.
In your sublunar shrine springs from Annwn
Pour a cauldron of infinite wisdom.
Daughters of Avalon dance at its ridge.
Their shadows twist to the roaring song.
I see you, white keeper of time and mist
Watching patiently beyond mortal bonds.
The moment rings clear as your guidance sure:
*Let the words be spoke and the path be walked.*

Hail Gwyn ap Nudd, King of Spirits!

# Hunter's Moon

Thinning the veil
from blue to silver
a goose with her flight
and murmurations at dusk
presage his opening
wagon ways, bridleways,
padways and fords
to the living past.

Through rain soaked night
and mist clad dawn
the hunt will ride
spirit paths
from primeval tracks
of tangled wild wood
to race with juggernauts,
baying for blood.

The hunt will ride
gauntlets of time.
Every soul knows
its hound's call.
From city's sleep
and junction's unrest
he will gather the dead
to the land of the living.

## Wagoner

There is a wagoner on the old ridge
Travelling from here to there
With a long stretch of road to traverse
And a fear of not coming home.

Reins slide drenched through his hands.
The swaying rump of his carthorse blurs.
His only light is the burning pipe
Clenched between teeth and an unknown end.

The wagon is empty of barrels
Yet their slosh and creak make rhyme
With hooves and wheels mired to this scene
As he travels a horse shoe of time

Eyes of the past look back at him.
His blinkered cob plods on.
A future unfolds in bright lit windows.
Hesitant cars emerge

To drive with ease down tarmac streets.
Fireworks burst over amber lights.
With a final throw of ember red
He casts away his pipe.

Hoof-falls fall much quieter
In the memory of mud.
Travelling from here to there
He knows he is not going home.

# The Region Linuis

*'Then it was that the magnanimous Arthur, with all the kings and military force of Britain, fought against the Saxons... The second, third, fourth and fifth (battles), were on another river, by the Britons called Duglas, in the region Linuis.'* – Nennius, *History of the Britons.*

In the region of endless water
I see blazoned in blue stillness
A raging sky of crimson
And a thousand crashing spears.

The host of Arthur's war band
Reap their slaughter of the Saxons.
In spirals scream the ravens
Round the deep and bloody lake.

Fierce the red maned chargers
Through the blue and flashing sword thrusts.
Quick their dancing footfalls
Through the thick and blood stained mud.

Harsh the clash of iron on iron,
Unheard the shriek of cloven flesh,
Unmarked the final rattling breath
When ravens scream over blood.

Dead the barren battlefield,
Empty the skies of ravens and red,
Silent the stars that shine in the staring
Eyes of slaughtered men.

Sad the song of the marching shades
Departing this land to the afterlife.
Still the blue and crimson lake.
Silent the blood stained sky.

*First published in *Heroic Fantasy Quarterly* (November 2013)

## Prayer for Netholme

I write this prayer for the white one
who loaned to me a mare of mist,
led me across the marsh of time
and granted me the seer's gift.

I write these words for the god
who led me through the rising mists
to find the lost island of Netholme
amidst the floating will o wisps.

I write these words from Netholme
looking across the rippling mere
to lights of halls and farmhouses
mixed with ghosts and flickering fear.

I write this prayer for Netholme,
forgotten island in the mist,
for the drained off mere, the bulrushes,
bitterns, cranes and fishermen.

I write this prayer for the souls
of the long forgotten dead
who greet us still in the fields,
wandering roads and haunted farmsteads.

I write these words for the guide
of the long forgotten dead
whose stories must be told
for future hope to live.

# Romany Rivers

Romany Rivers is a British born Witch, Reiki Master and Artist living in Canada, exploring a life of personal passion, spirituality and creativity. An advocate for healing and self realization through art, poetry and the written word, she works within her local community encouraging others to discover their spirituality and personal truth through creative endeavors. Author of *Poison Pen Letters to Myself* and *The Woven Word: A Book of Invocations and Inspirations*, Romany is also a regular contributor to various magazines, blogs, poetry anthologies and Pagan community books. When not writing, creating or running around after two energetic children, Romany turns her hand to individual healing sessions and community projects that provide family support.

## Imbolc

Deep in the belly of the earth life now stirs
Awakening within and shaking free of ice and snow
The Goddess carries the child of promise within her arms
Trailing light and warmth wherever he goes
Slowly the world awakens from its slumber
Pushing shadows back from long cold night
All around
Life abounds
Reaching out towards the growing light

## Imbolc Festival of Light

Welcome to the festival of light
Where springtime lies within our sight
Earth softens and milk flows
Babies are born, seeds are sown
Soon the thaws will flood the streams
And winter becomes the land of dreams
The Crone returns to the land of snow
And all around us light now grows
Hold high your flame, shine your light
Chase back the shadows and shrinking night
Prepare the path for spring to come
And rejoice now in the growing sun!

# Scry the Becoming

The reflection of the Divine
I look into your eyes
And see all that does not exist
I look into the Divine
Into the knowing eyes
And see that I do not exist, do not resist, do not become
I am you
You are me
I am one within all
All within one
I am the spiral of order
In the divine chaos
I am the chaos
Unravelled
Undone
The reflection infinite
Contained and formed
By the boundary of understanding
The reflection of the Divine
I look into your eyes
And see all that has or will exist
I exist, I resist, I am becoming
I am you
You are me
I am made whole once more
As one within the All
Slowly I become
The reflection in blackened glass
Looking out at the Divine
Looking in at me

# Touching Divine

A god to me
Divine male incarnate
Filling my eyes with potentiality
Narrowing my vision until all that remains is you
Beyond place
Beyond time
Beyond world of flesh or dream
Somewhere in between
I meet you there
You hail me as goddess
Not unreal, not mythical, but divine and human
With belly full of baby scars
Eyes surrounded with laughter lines
And hair kissed with winters touch
Goddess still I am
And it is true to me, in honesty, in beauty
For I am divine in your eyes
As you are in mine
I raise a hand of time gone by
Brush a hair from your eyes
And touch the wonder of masculine divine
My path to God through your heart
Your path to Goddess through mine

## Surrender

Chaos, Creation,
Confusion, elation
Spinning cycles of power and peace
Standing naked in the storm
Exposed and vulnerable
Battered and battling
Being
Birthing
At every single moment
Every possibility collapsing into this
This one moment
This one moment
This one moment
That never ends, always begins
Surrounded by the movement and din
Impossible to move outside of it all
Instead I move in
Towards my centre
Huddling my tired form
Deep into the storm
And suddenly I can breathe
There is space and silence at the centre
I raise my hands to the sky
Stand tall
Stand back
Observe my life as it whips on by
This is me
All me
The creation, the destruction
The chaos, the peace
The pleasure, the grief
All me

This is my storm
I surrender to myself
And wail into the winds of change and circumstance
All of my own making
Each echoed scream reflecting
The possibilities
The probabilities
That collapse into this
One
Moment

## Oceans Deep

There is fear at the surface
The panic driven resistance of stubborn survival
Of denial
The downward spiral
Exhausted, tired, fearful and numb
Constantly looking up and beyond
Refusing to gaze into the depths
Lest the deep darkness claims me as its own
But claim me it does
When I am too tired to fight for air
Beyond numb despair
Beyond fear
I sink below the surface
In cold acceptance of all that I have denied
And resistance leaves my form
I relax into the unknown
Letting it carry the weight of my heart
And suddenly there is peace
I pause, held, floating
And all around me are the thoughts and feelings I held beneath
the surface
The aspects of myself that lapped at the shores of my soul
The ebb and flow of acceptance and resistance
It is all here
All encompassing
The depths of a person
Oceans deep
Unfathomable in one lifetime
Unchartered waters not yet seen, not yet experienced, not yet
understood
A desire to explore the unknown jolts new life into a tired heart
My body electrified and inspired to move

No longer denying the depths
Below me the tidal emotions push and pull
Each movement a slippery stepping stone to the surface
Above me the sun reflects upon the water
And for the first time in forever
I can see the light that shines upon me
I reach out
Break the surface
Buoyed by the depths of my feelings
Surrounded by the shifting, sparkling reflections of a new dawn
With fresh perspective
I balance upon the waters of my heart
And lift my face towards the light

# First Days

When you were born
I lived in days so dark
That your little light only deepened the shadows
Made the dark corners of my mind heavy and visceral
I loved you
Fiercely
With a heart that expanded and bruised with every gaze
As my heart swelled
My mind shrank
Into fear and sadness and loneliness and grief
I loved you
Overwhelmingly
With every fibre of my being
But that love seemed out of reach
Far beyond my reaching fingertips
Across the chasm of my soul
Across the abyss of my mind
I loved you
Completely
Yet could not create a pathway between loss and love
Holding you close brought aching pain
I drowned in tears and shame
So much shame
How could I fail you so in your first days?
How could I grieve at a time of joy?
I would look to your father
Beseeching
Needing
Holding you forth
Blaming myself for feeling blessed relief
When he took you from my arms
And I hid my face behind empty hands

Oh but I loved you
Intensely
I watched you grow
And my love grew
And your light grew
Chasing away the darkness without my awareness
Like the gradual dawn after a long night
My world slowly shifting
From dark to grey
To better days

## Stolen Seconds

Sometimes I steal into the garden
And stand by the washing line
Laundry forgotten in my hands as my eyes search the skies
Looking for something
Seeing everything
Noticing nothing
I breathe deeply
And release one long shuddering sigh
A breath held without conscious thought
Waiting for just a few minutes peace to fly free from the
constricted chest
I look down
At my trembling hands
Clutching tiny clothes
Representations of the miniature people
Who take up enormous space within my daily life
Leaving little room for me as I shrink and shrivel to give them
more room
I let go
Of the laundry
Of the breath
Of the stress
Of the tiredness
Of the constant needing, feeding, reading, singing, sighing,
playing and praying for peace
I let go
And close my eyes
Wondering if tears will kiss my cheeks in gratitude
For the silent still moments
Stolen swiftly
Beside the washing line

## Autumn Arrives

Autumn arrives
As my son cries
And places fallen leaf upon my outstretched fingertips
Fix the tree he pleads
The leaf
It fell over
Fix the tree
If only it were so simple
To kiss it better
To hug away the hurt
To ease the seasons sorrow
I wonder if his heart will break a little
With every red gold shiver
With every bitter breeze
With every leaf crunching underfoot
The tree is broken in his mind
How does one explain
The time and tides
The ebb and flow
The come and go
To brimming tear filled brown eyes?
Is it too hard a truth to learn so young
That some things cannot be undone?
I cannot fix the tree for him
And reality upon me dawns
Just as the time has come for leaves to change
The mighty Mama also falls
No longer magic touch
Healing all with simple love
There are things in life beyond a Mamas reach
She cannot even fix the tree

# Martin Pallot

Martin Pallot has been writing poetry since the early eighties, mainly inspired by Nature and his pagan beliefs. Over the years, he has had some success, seeing poems published on-line and in print, both here and in America.

He loves to read old books of topography and history and the folklore, myths and legends of our ancestors, all of which have provided inspiration in the past. He is fascinated by the sounds and rhythms of words, the labyrinthine etymology of language and the naming of places within the landscape, some of which are at least as strange as fiction. He also admires the early poets and tale tellers and the way they engaged the ear, as well as the mind of their audience.

One consequence of all this is that he tries to use things like word play, alliteration and assonance in his work, not only to help tell the story and write the picture but hopefully to encourage people to try saying the poetry as well as just reading it, whether it's a longer, more discursive poem like *Faerie Tales,* or brief, controlled pieces like the selections of Haiku and Tanka included here.

# Winter Song

Stark the sight seems,
Iron hard the earth hold of this solstice time,
The joy of seasons past, gone down to dust
Beneath the gasping grasp of cold.

The world, suspended in a snow drift,
Sleeps away the sun starved winter wait,
Water cracks beneath the weight of frozen air,
Trees stand withered in the north born wind;
Life is but a shudder of its former self.

Yet still the life persists,

The robin sings his song of hollow hills,
Fox tracks dance across the frosty ground,
Snowflakes whisper secrets as they fall,
The ever green man still shows his face
And listens,
For the mother's heart, that barely beats;
But does.

# Imbolc

This path leads softly
To the solace of snowdrops.

The carpet of snow is threadbare,
Cob webbed weavings
Of frozen water, seem to wait
A change of wind
To waft away.

Sunlight shivers
In the eastern sky,
And spreads across
The goose grey winter clouds.
But now, its strength
Begins to grow
With every turning of the earth,
And calls to the sleeping seed
To spite the ice,
And bring its blessing
To the waking world.

The milk of spring,
Begins to flow across the land.

The wind is changing.

## Spring Song

The deosil dance of the waxing year,
Brings the seed to birth,
As warmth drives out old winter's fear
And melts the heart of earth.

Raise up the lord of all that's green
And give him room to breathe,
Let him wake from winter's dream
To bless the budding leaves.

Let the maiden see her love
And greet him with a kiss,
Let them twine in oaken grove
To bring each other bliss.

Let earth and sun and wind and rain
Be fertile in their way,
As spring reclaims her old domain,
And life comes out to play.

## Bluebells

They do not need
Some gods graffiti
To mark their beauty,
Beneath the boughs
Of a gold bright
May day morning.

The sun green leaf shade,
On the blue
And wind waved
Bells,
Creates a sea,
On which the longships
Of the fae
Might journey forth
To far Annwn.

Oceanic undulations.

Lapping waves,
Against a distant beech.

# Haiku

Fox track in damp earth,
A plethora of feathers
Where he broke his fast.

Awaiting sunrise,
Mist gathers in the hollows,
Day begins to breathe.

Face of granite cracked
At the waking of the world,
When volcanoes yawned.

The sun is rising,
The pipes of Pan are sounding
From a thousand throats.

Velvet burrower,
Blind hunter in the darkness,
Creating mountains.

Beneath the shade, and
Feather fall of willow branch,
My mind and I, drift.

Selkie and her seal,
Two souls in a single skin.
Neither can be held.

Sculpted by the night,
And moon light, clouds drift above
Like ancient ice flows.

# Tanka

Eagles eerie cries,
Echo from its high eyrie.
Mountain shares the song,
Sending warning to the world,
Wind weaver, Sky Wolf, Eagle.

Fox under an oak,
Watches the full moon rising.
Staring up on high,
At the fox eye in the sky.
The mighty Vixen, Mother.

In Silver Birch wood,
Do I see you, russet one?
Or is it the leaves
Dancing on the westing wind,
Call your shape to my minds eye?

A sunlit forest,
Woodpecker makes his magic,
Calling to the storm.
Thunder drums are answering,
Scaring brightness from the sky.

Owl and Butterfly,
Singing songs of moon and sun,
Ancient melodies.
Spirit hears the flight of words,
Whispering on their wing tips.

Spring is eyeing me,
Looking out to see what stirs.
Ready to hare off,
Leading me a merry dance
Across the fields of Summer.

## Wolf Voice

Wolf, howling to the moon.
The wind hears your words,
The earth feels your voice.
Sending out your spirit sound,
Calling to the great She wolf
Who shakes the stars from her fur.

Loping in the light of her one great eye,
Silver, shadowing the pack path.
Snow, scented by the passing prey,
Guides you on your killing way.
The trackless whiteness,
Sculpted by spirits of the air,
Into shape of deer and bison.
These insubstantial ghosts,
A pulsing presence in your
Preternatural eye.

When the kill is made,
The pack song rises,
To thank the She Wolf
For her gift of life,
To the den of generations.

And the moon,
Resting on a bed
Of winter branches,
Smiles, to hear
The voice of Wolf.

## Sun After Rain

The effervescent
Emerald shimmer
Of the breeze
Among the leaves,
As the sun
Plays hide and seek
Around the clouds.

And a shower of crows
Shake open their wings
To the lift and sweep
Of the wind,
Above the branches
Of beech and birch;
Where sunlight slants,
Raising lights
Of coffee, brown and gold,
Upon the darkened damp
Of mast and mold.

# Puck

Hedgerow Halfling,
Born of both worlds
With a dancing foot in each.

Feasting on the fruits
Of hazel tree and hive,
Quaffing foaming acorn cups
Of beer and buttermilk.

Shadow hopping
In a mouse skin cloak,
Or riding through the night
Upon a screech owl,
You watch our ways
From season to season,
Within the circle
Of the passing year.

Your antlered alter ego
Slipping between the trees
On long mid-summer eves.

Spirit of both path and hearth,
You doze away the winter
Safe within the cob webbed corner
Of the Inglenook.

And have the greatest love of humankind
Of all the folk who dwell in hallowed hills.

An ancient Briton, brother to old Brock,
Riding on his burly back
Along the hollow track.

You counted Aveburys' standing stones
The day the builders left.

Helped to light the bonefires
That warned of Caesars might.

And saw the fatal arrow
Find its mark on Senlac hill.

A woodland wisdom,
Green hearted, hooded man,
You were a force to count on
In those, straightforward days,
When there where more of you
And less of us.

But then the cities grew,
And threw you back with all your kind
Out of mind,
Into our myth
And nursery rhyme.

And so we gave you,
In our foolishness,
A foxglove dunce's cap,
So we could laugh
Around our urban hearth,
At your madcap mischief.

And give no thought,
To what might lie,
Around the corner of our eye,
Within the darkling wood.

## Faerie Tales

When I was young, as now I'm not,
I read a feast of faerie tales,
Of castles built on craggy rocks
And pirate ships with silver sails,

Of maidens, heroes, goblins grim
And treasure held by dragon's whim.

"Come now my fine one, step into the faerie ring."
The one with the looking glass in it,
It will show you what's behind you,
(which some say is the future).

My mother said I never should
Talk to strange folk in the wood,
But grandma said – and this quite rightly,
All might be well if I spoke politely.

Beware:
Those men with beard so blue,
Or those who have a vulpine air.

Locked rooms at tower tops
And pools so deep and still.

Food that tells you to eat it,
Or cats with cheesy grins.

If you should follow the spiral path,
That leads into the hollow hill,
Be sure it's no unseelie rath,
Where you'll be kept against your will.

The queen of the dark elves,
Has a necklace made of broken promises,

Rubies the colour of regret,
Emeralds the colour of expectation,
Sapphires the colour of sorrow,
Diamonds the colour of despair,
Each stone
The shape of a soft sigh.
All hung, upon on a cord
Of twisted meanings.

Go out upon midsummer eve,
And soon in faeries you'll believe,
Go out again on hallowe'en,
You'll see things that should not be seen

Have you seen a silky selkie
Shed her skin beneath the moon.

Or the golden gleam of sunlight,
On a stone engraved with runes.

Some graven wyrd stone
Of the elven realms,
That tells a tale from misted time,
Shrouded in a Dragon's breath.
An ancient monsters questing war
Full of bile and fires wrath.
And the war band, strong in shield wall, who
Did not flinch from fates iron path.

Once upon a time the woods that walled us round,
Were home to fearsome fetches and shadow shaping dread,
But then our knowledge grew and burst the woodland bound,
Now all that's left to fear is the beast beneath the bed.

These tales all came from out the beech,
Or boc as once those trees were known,
Which now is book to you and me
And still these tales I've not outgrown.
Now if I sit and read awhile,
The trees surround me still,
And even after all these years,
I've yet to have my fill.

# Beverley Price

Beverley Price is a weaver of dark prose and poetry, dreamer of Gothic imagery, cat lover and nature worshipper. Her work deals with the bitter fact that love is not always chocolate boxes and roses mixed in with the imagery of her pagan roots and love of mythology. She has been published in several poetry anthologies as well as being a published poet in her own right.

# In the moonlight

On the way to Avalon I saw you there,
It was somewhere past twelve o'clock.
I stood there with my cold hard heart,
And skies slowly filled with furry bats.
I craved for something so much more,
I did not want to be alone to blasphemy.
You were my bad obsession, falling away,
Karma lead me to the Isle of apples.
Once upon a time, this benevolent fairy,
Did not want this vengeance of dark magic,
Or this pain in her soul, the song of all-times.
Yet here in my place of blissful harmony,
As I am about to take the moon boat home.
You stand there on the path I am about to walk,
I was your calling, more than a cute friend.
Together we created a creaked love story,
My beloved backstabber in a prison of dreams.
Fallen whispers crash down like Icarus,
Nevermore I will be the sole sorceress of Avalon.
The portal of my desolation and healing,
The place that was soft, dark and dreamless.
The place that ended all my memories,
I tried to share it with you in good company.
The pain of being apart is like crimson butterflies,
Fluttering about like a white bird with Autumnal spirit.
In the end close up, was it nothing but an illusion?
All fake smiles, and broken lullabies,
I really can not make you love me.
Morgana the shape changer, it is show-time,
As I become a moth attracted to your flame.
Your beautiful lies, and I have opened my eyes,
I will be your silken enchantress, the knight's lady.

Imagine the day after tomorrow underwater,
On the Autumnal metamorphoses one last breath.
With hopeless reflections of infinity of maybe loneliness,
As the moth, I will look for myself on the Isle.
My own enchanted garden amongst the mist of Avalon,
One summer night, when I am no longer a bitch.
And if you can get there, amongst the apple blossoms,
Before the clocks tick my life away.
And the rest of me becomes an angel,
Tell me the truth about your feelings.

# The Lilith Effect

You land as gently as a butterfly.
Your concept is as a heartless bitch.
You will be there at the Apocalypse.
Take your rightful place as a Goddess.
As the night begins to slowly crawl.
The darkest hour you begin to tease.
Embracing the cold whispers of huluppu.
Inconceivable loved as a source of hurt.
Queen of the night, darkness and pain.
Keeper of the moons sorrows and secrets.
I'll pretend on this night of the witches.
That you are sending your love to me.
Still here waiting for you not to suffer.
I won't leave you here alone my angel.
Something is still missing, a nightly lover.
Bury you deep inside me, sweet angel of death.
Around that corner, will you follow me?
Without a child it is easier to fly.
Without a mother it is harmony.
In the ice cold of loneliness.
Under the huluppu tree we sinned.
The Eve of bones, we became saints.
A whiter shade of pale singing dark songs.
You make me see the light, stand my ground.
I will follow and haunt your owls.
Sweet bloody kisses, I am not ashamed,
To say that I am alone and waiting for you.

# A Winters Heart

I have a winters' heart
For me, a special part.
Snowflakes causes smiles
A whiteness that goes on for miles.
I run through holly
Coldness makes me jolly.
Red berries I'd want to kiss
Summertime I'd give a miss.
The season gives me love
Amongst the whiteness of a dove.
Bleakness that makes me feel at home
A world encapsulated in a snow dome.
A feeling deep within my soul
And as Sacred as mistletoe.
Eternally waiting for Yule
The Holly and Oak king duel.
Royalty waiting for an empire
A partner to take me higher.
This season leaves its mark
Rough like oak tree bark.
Bitter berries that taste sweet
A love of coldness over heat.
Minutes go by too fast
A season that will not last.
But a man come one winter night
Destined to turn me to the light.
Come to disturb my darkly plan
A God in disguise as a man.
He only took me partly the way
But I will reach the sunshine one day.

## Echoes of Love

You led me to the place where hemlock meets the oak.
By the amber waters of Babylon.
A place full of the whispers of love.
And the blazing screams of banging hate.
The wind speaks of maddening possession.
It batters me without any mercy.
And dances about me like an evil ballerina.
It is filled with hateful intention.
A burning flame tells tales of mystery ways.
It burns with violent cruelty and breaking dawns.
As I remember that I was never good.
Passions that was deemed as immoral.
The winding river sings that I can live.
That she would never give up on me.
A mere taste would keep me young forever.
I know that she wants to possess me.
The earth is narrating tales of tragedy.
Its deep, dark soil is up to no good.
It seems to conspire to take me away.
It is ingraining into every groove.
It tells my heart that it is a fool.
My spirit shrieks a warning like a crow.
I need to make it out of here alive.
It rebels against the songs of passion.
It cried that I need to flee this place.
I turn to you to fire the killing blow.
I realise the words I hear are not yours.
But echoes of love that died many years ago.
In this place, hemlock and oak weeps.
Here, the amber waters are on fire.
And yet I am here, still waiting.
Air wants it their way, fire turns to stars.

Water keeps on living, earth is stricken.
Between us there are flying sparks.
I want to be the first thing you see.
You take me in your arms and kiss me.
Your kisses opened up Pandora's Box.
Leaving me with nothing but tuneful hope.
You take my hand and lead me from this place.
A place that holds nothing but echoes of dead love.

# Phoenix reborn

Another one of my many dreams,
A bird with wings magnificent and vast.
Being consumed on a fiery pyre,
Watching the phoenix come to past.
It noted my arrival and the tale to be told,
My loved ones reveal themselves to me.
Only you made me feel this loved,
Remember, look for the phoenix in all you see.
My pale, haggard lips part to form a smile,
The winds were cold, but the phoenix is safe.
Even as it turned to desensitised dust,
Do not fear the survival of this tiny waif.
A single feather lies on my back,
Reminding me that I can take all of that.
Chained to the wall with my depression,
Tears that were shed from careless chat.
Dying a thousand times only to be reborn,
Until the silver flamed fires fill the skies.
Consuming the dying trapping brambles,
Taking from you compassion, my prize.
You have given me a strong fight,
To live to hear your beckoning call.
To rise again from that same pyre,
Yet I have no energy, forced to crawl.
You forced the new being out of me, light into dark,
Just to be relived of the wicked thing I once did.
The dark skies are immediately illuminated,
The past does not matter now, my final bid.
For freedom, a life, a phoenix reborn.

# Hecate's way

On a dark and stormy night.
Scentless fields are in shade
Hecate's darkness gracing the land.
Should I play her maid?

I wish that I could be insane.
Are you lightening the fairies flight?
You work with the wind
I raise my eyes to your darken sight.

Hecate, you are the mysteries unknown.
And has the wideness of the seas.
A dark singer of the crossroads.
The sober sorceress of all she sees.

Word that I have that you are wild.
You are why I still dwell.
In the new dawn, my eyes will see.
Light escaping from this dead hell.

## Winter is...

Winter, the trees stand bare.
Snow covers the ground.
A secret message, just for me to share.
It died on the breeze, not making a sound.

Blunted by the whitewash.
Reinforcing my desire.
Whisper leaves, the story told.
The urge to feel and enquire.

The winter wolves are coming.
I would love to be there.
And round about, the weight of time.
This winter is usual and rare.

Now, winter time is full of light.
Winter has become my lover.
Your love murmurs to me in winter.
Hot with your love, and summer to discover.

# Clock time

Hopes are high my Autumn Queen,
For a Cadillac and haunted home.
You, Snow Queen is my original sin,
Butterflies became my binding comb.
Fading away like a dead line,
The widow is shivering, howling.
Don't forget my Queen of fire,
The soul of swans is prowling.
In the spooky wonderland of moondust,
Honour me and my nightshift purity.
Angel of the afterlife is frozen.
The last butterfly garden, my security.
The mystery of the black swan,
Is the masquerade of escaping Hell.
Once I was the one who could love,
Daisies in my hair and I am a belle.
The silence of the moon spirit,
Spooky Valentines are the gravity of loves.
I am a vamp far away from you,
Butterflies that turn into colourblind doves.
Sweet nightmare in the forests of denial,
When it hurts that I am burning.
Elixir leads to dark vanity on fake wings,
The death of this swan is beyond yearning.
This blind witch dances in pink Autumn,
The ruins of the forest told me of your lies.
Missing people are usually spirit eaters,
Got a feeling of illusions of skies.
A melody of self-destruction, fallen angel,
The sacrifice would be my burning heart.
The carnival is over, this is the last song,
Lilith is by the eating tree making art.

Exit are the tears of the underworld,
Maleficent, cardinal, my heart is dying.
The rooms of windows show the midnight ride,
White nights, my spider witch is crying.
Garlands presents a cold presence,
Bubbles of freedom become a fairy.
Butterflies taste of death, call me name,
Beauty of life is sweet as a cherry.
Heaven on earth was never was or will be,
Take my life and save my soul.
Kingdom of emptiness full of blue fish,
The room of silence I take a stroll.
Your signs show a mermaid in distress,
Sounds of spring sings a dreamy farewell.
Heart of this fairytale is your ghost,
Faded is the bubbles of a rebel.
Soul sister with a spirit of freedom,
Tears of a razorblade angel is my sin.
In the year of the tiger, hawthorn month,
The reflection of death stole everything.
You stole my heart, memories won't fade,
Valentine white was the soul stealer.
Fallen was the Goddess of the abyss,
Vampire hearted and yet a healer.
Evanescent mind causes the break down.
Fallen angel hears the sounds of the night.
Lotus flower is dead and yet divine,
Survivor that is still in love with the light.
Wonderland homes the black winged angel,
In the mystic night, you belong to me.
Meeting fear is beyond sorcery and theft.
Forest nymph is unable to feel and flee.
Eternally yours is this cold love,
Voodoo girl has the soul of a fighter.

Lament, dark mother queen, that midnight song,
Snow white queen, can you get much brighter?
Paradise city lit by the magic of candles,
You and I are martyrs for love.
Unread snowflakes are a cause of envy,
Fire Goddess, the bleeding of a dove.
Erosion of the sultry blue seduction,
My dark land is my gift to give.
Shadows and darkness are unleased,
Damned and divine is how I live.
Snow white with a white hyperfast soul,
The blessing is in black birds.
Nowhere land has the magic inside,
Wish you were here and to say the words.
Make a wish unless you are a snow queen,
End of words at the enchanted forest.
Heart of snow drowned in jaded sorrow,
Blue marsh is the face of a florist.
A drowning girl in a secret place,
Awaiting you, tears of the jester saint.
Dark angel frozen in a sleeping ocean,
Welcome to Avalon with its haunted taint.
Nostalgically I thought of lost dreams,
Winter romance by the magic of the moon.
Sisters of the night are my ego,
Elvish forest, dark side of the tune.
Violin dreams walk on to heaven,
Sisterhood alone amongst the rosy trees.
Insomniac to the bitter end,
But make me unhurtable please?

MOON

BOOKS

Moon Books invites you to begin or deepen your encounter with Paganism, in all its rich, creative, flourishing forms.